GEOMETRICAL DESIGN
Coloring Book

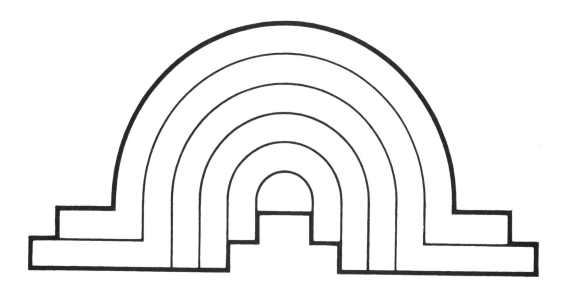

SPYROS HOREMIS

ABOUT THIS BOOK

At first glance, some of the designs in this book may look very complicated. However, you will quickly discover that each one is made up of combinations of repeated shapes and parts. In each case you are free, of course, to use color to highlight any aspect of the design that interests you. Some you may wish to tone down with a quiet and simple color scheme; others you may want to make as exciting and brilliant as a flashing neon sign. Whatever approach you choose, you can be sure that the finished picture will be uniquely your own.

1

2

3

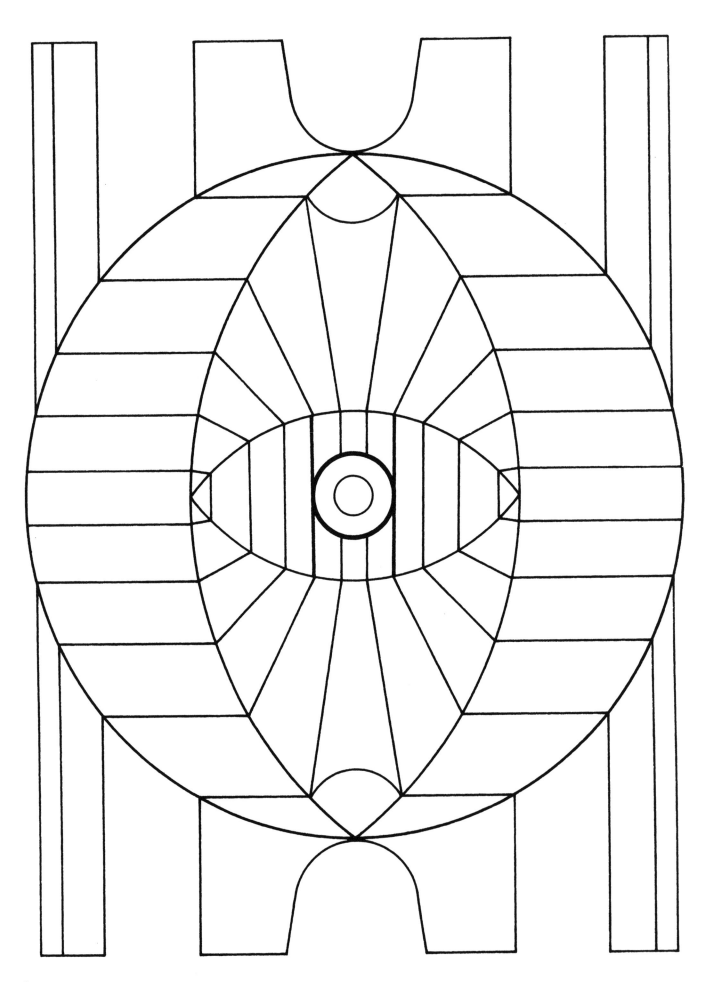

4

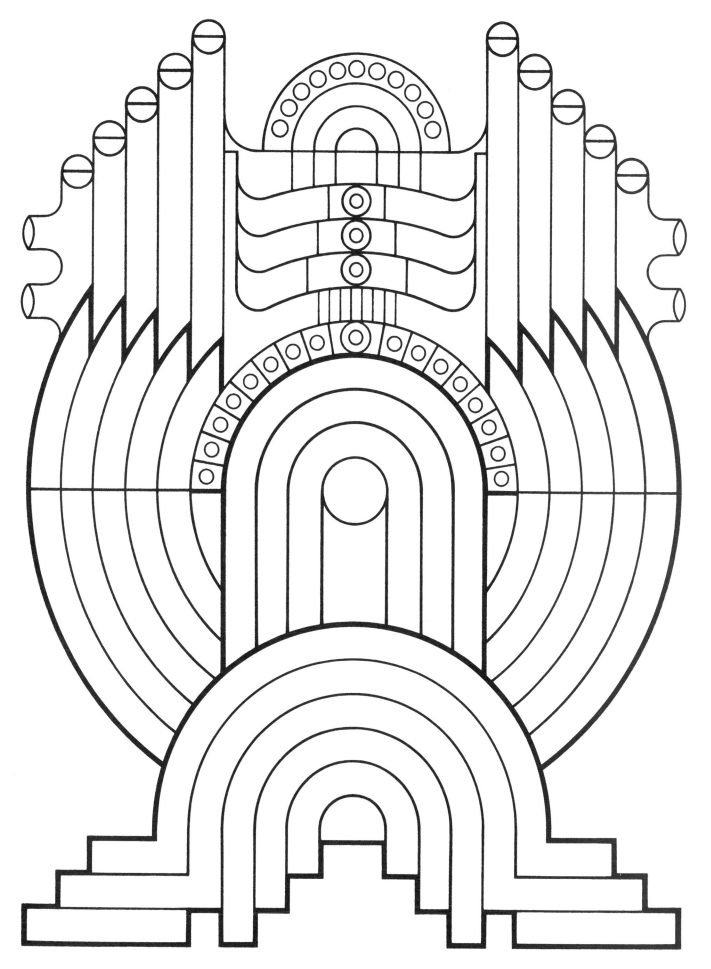

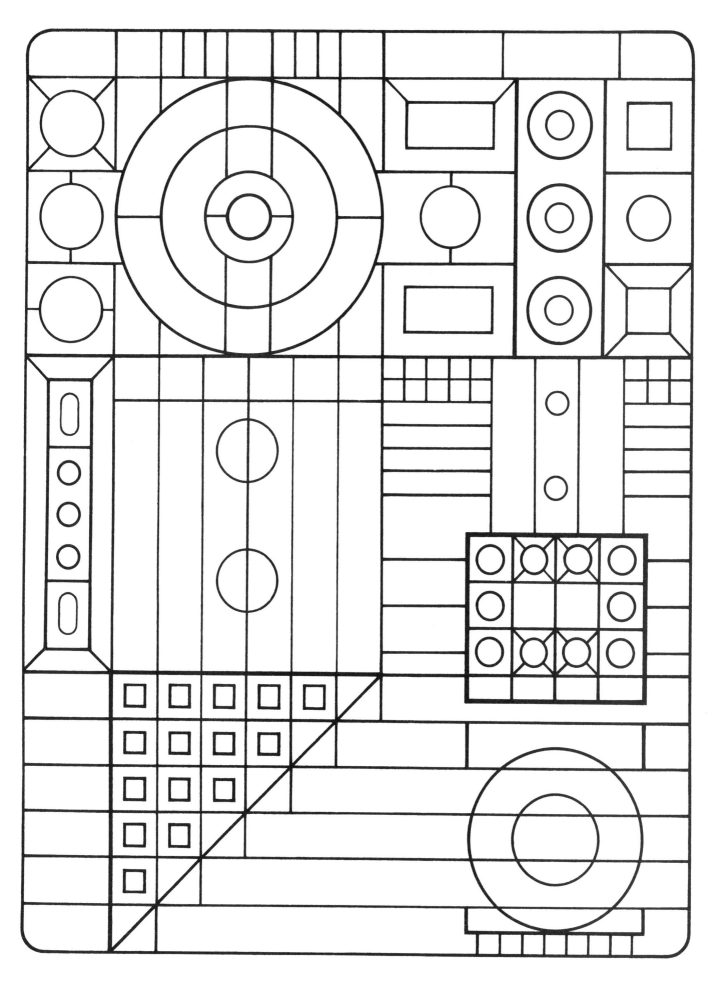

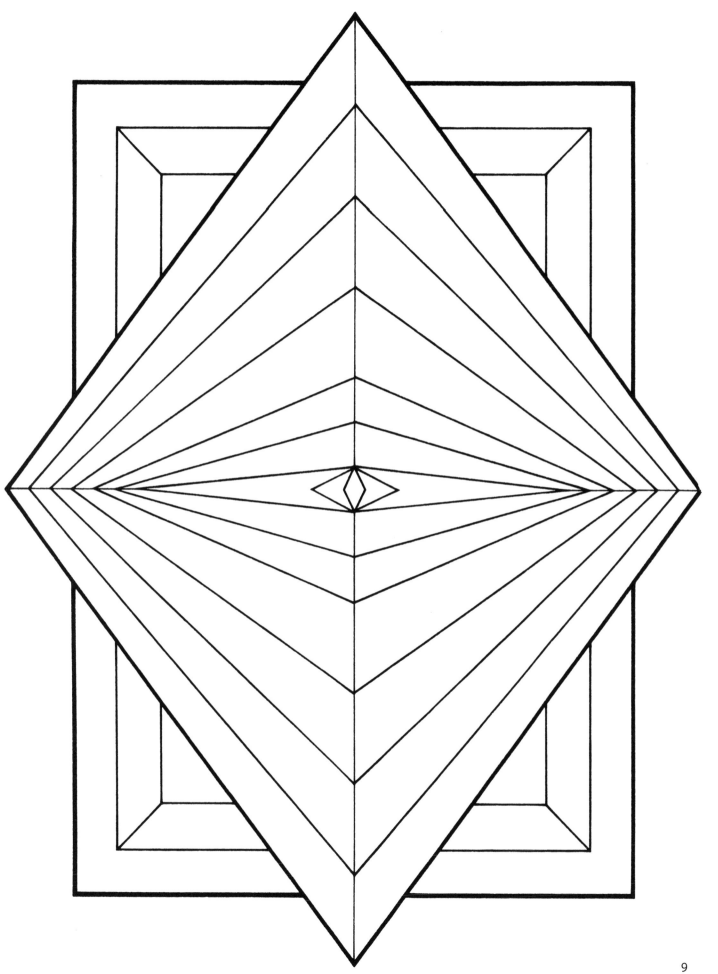

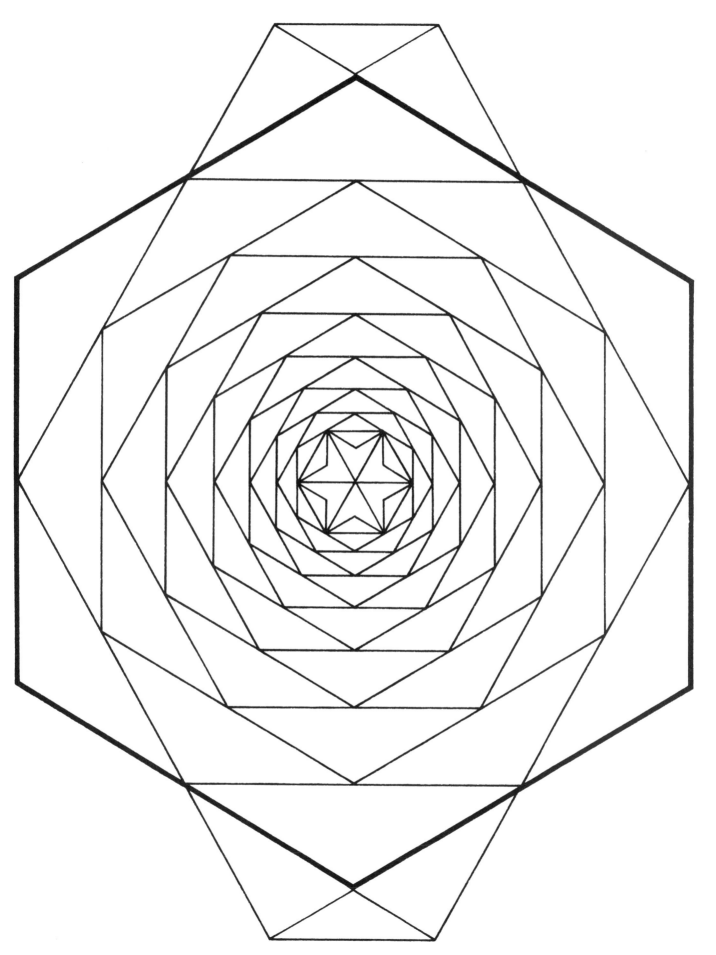

11

13

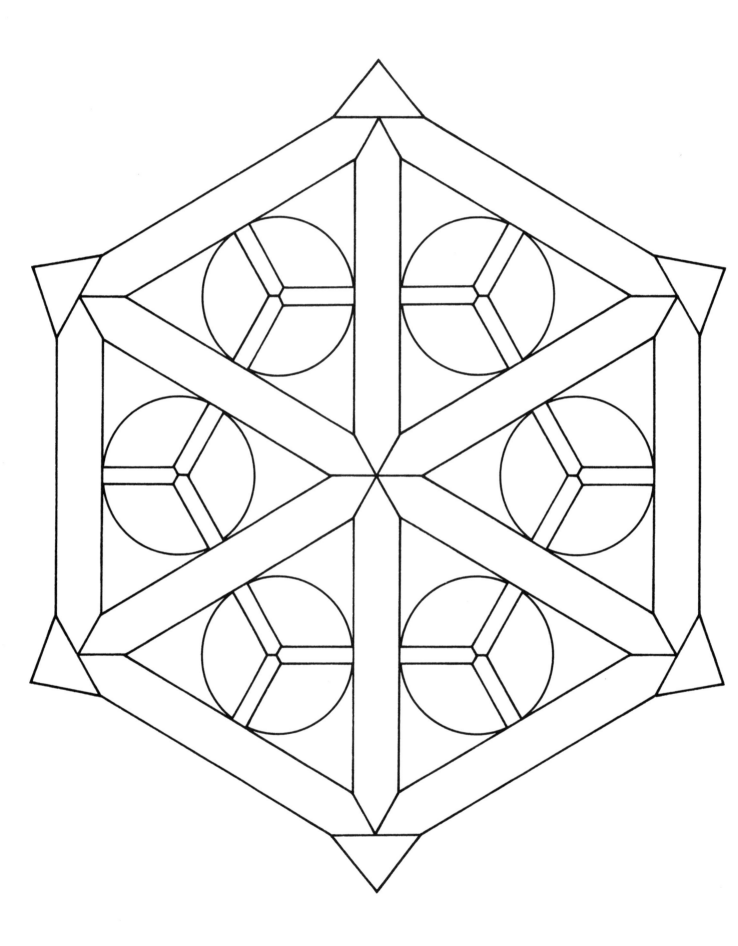

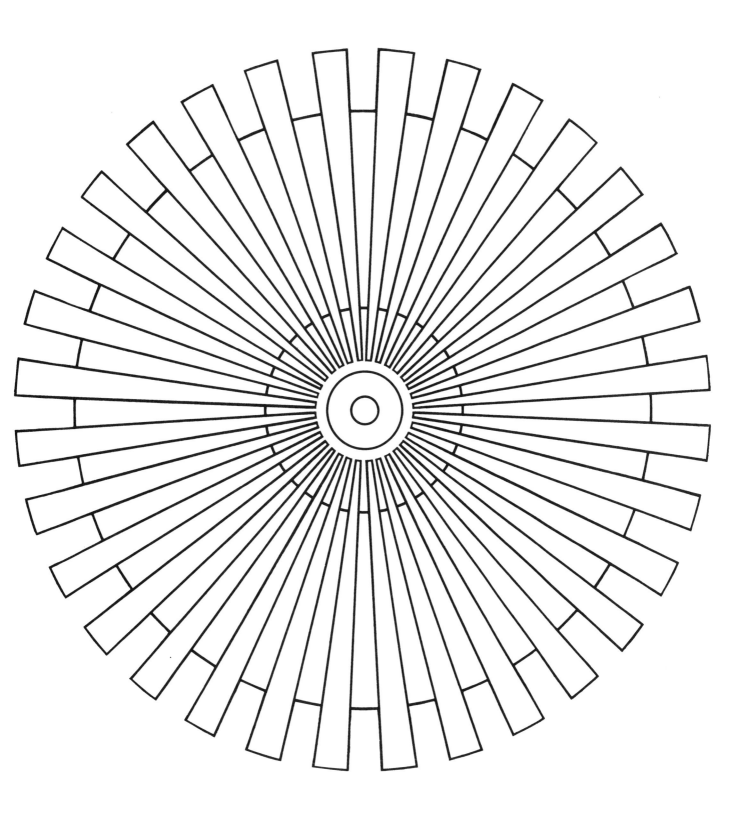

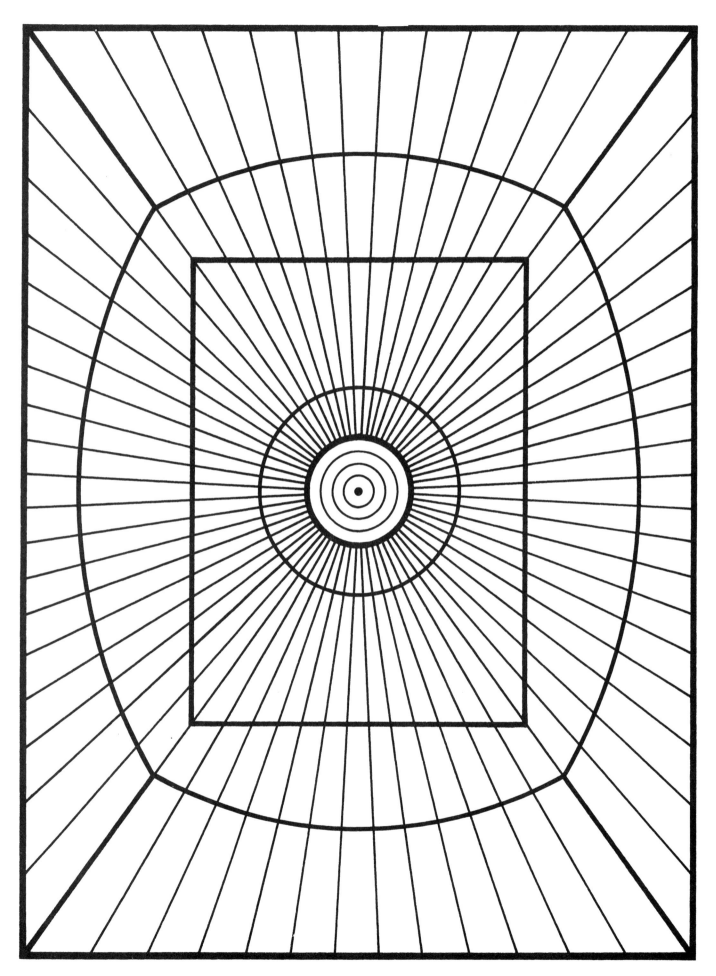

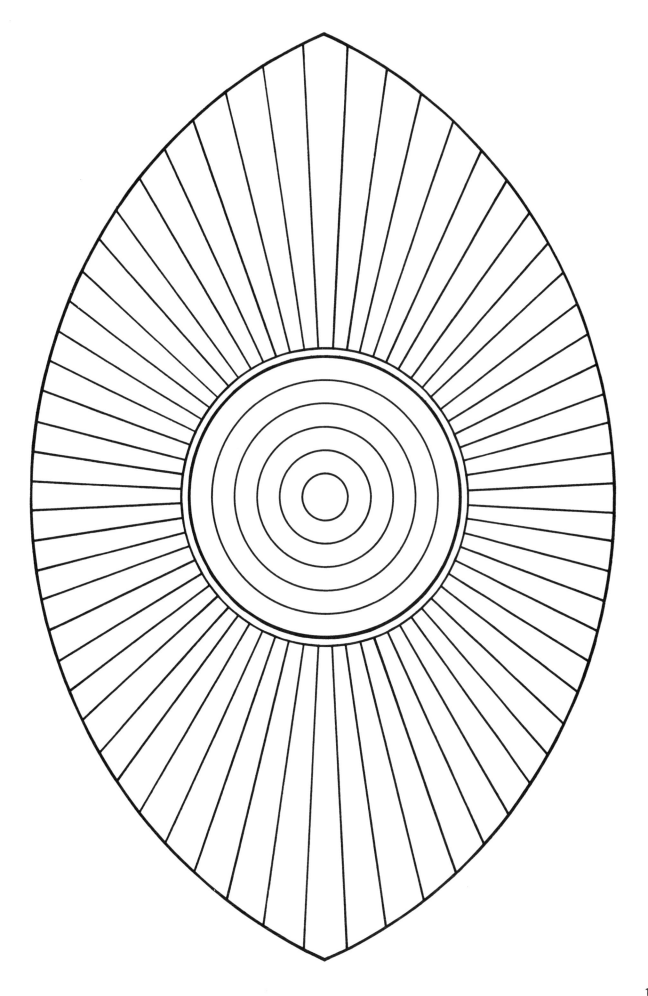

22

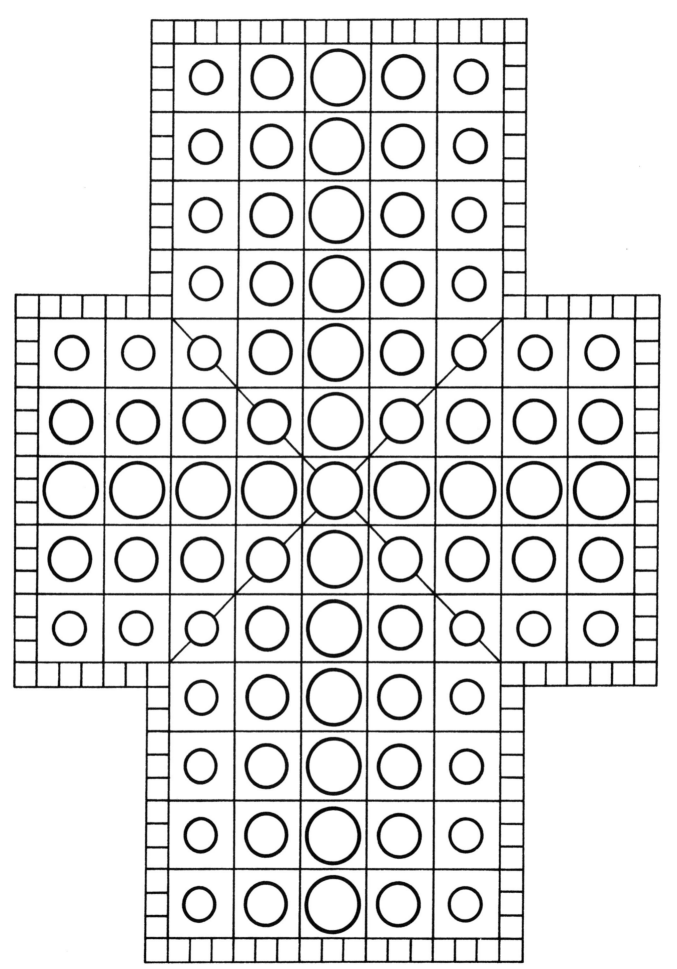

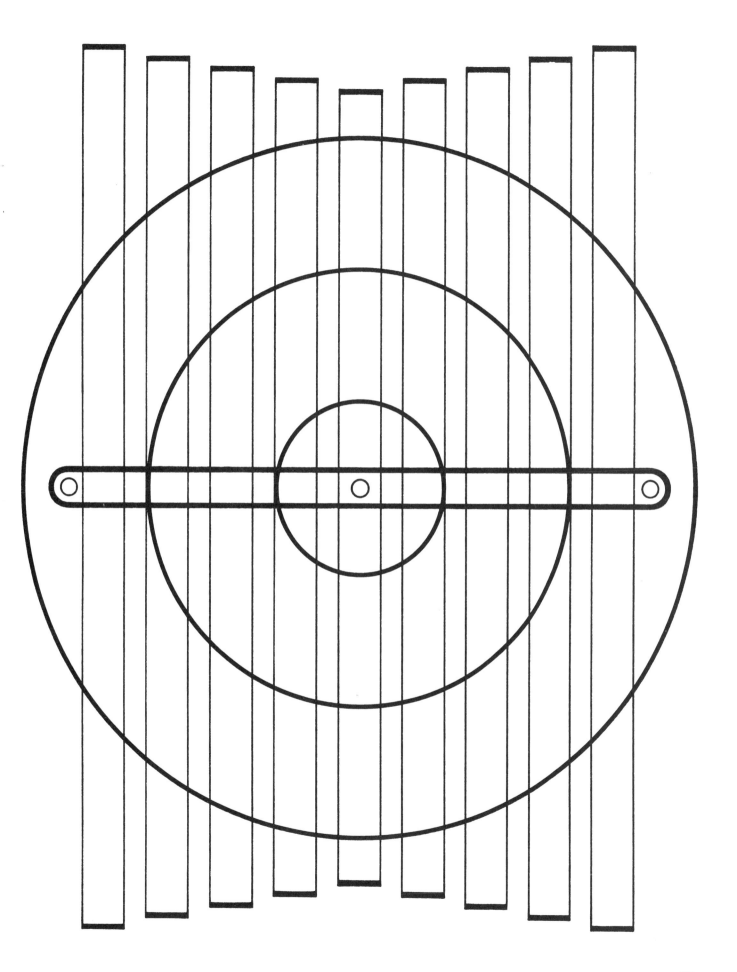

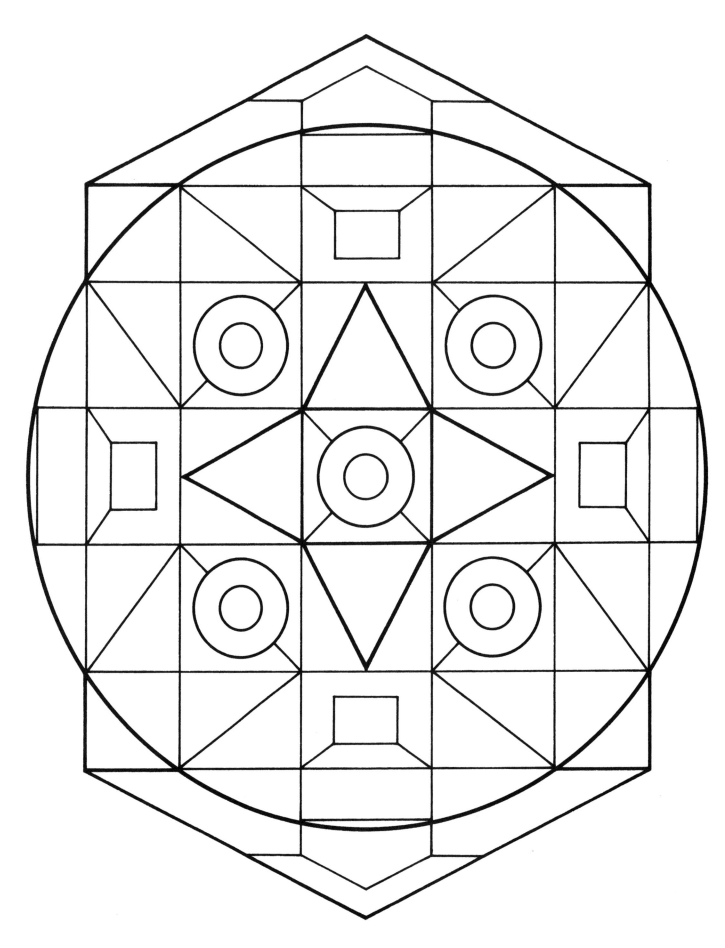

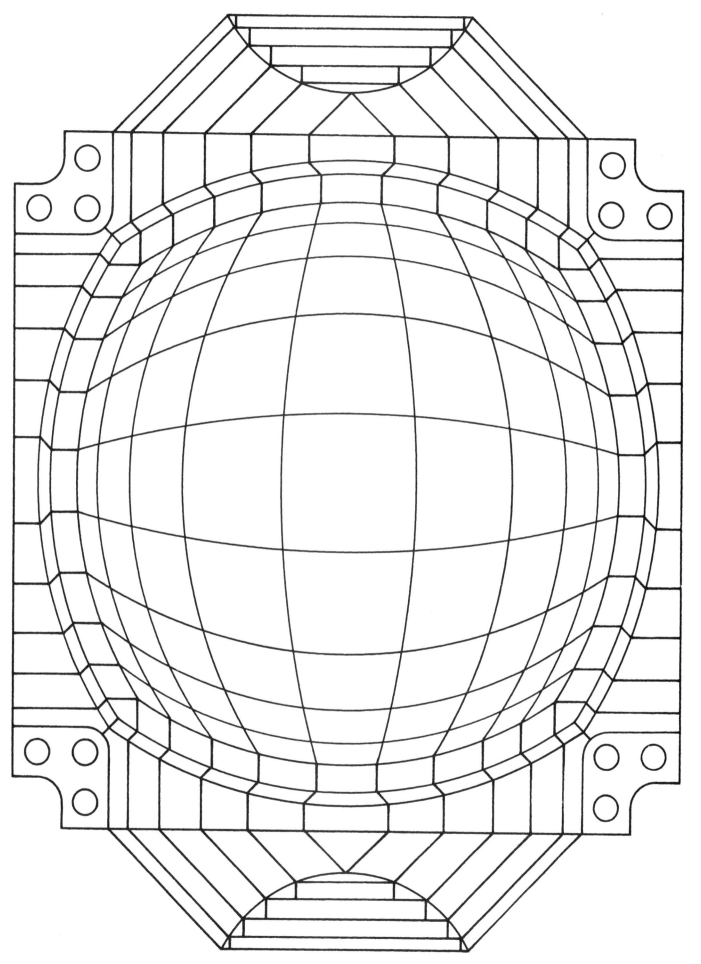

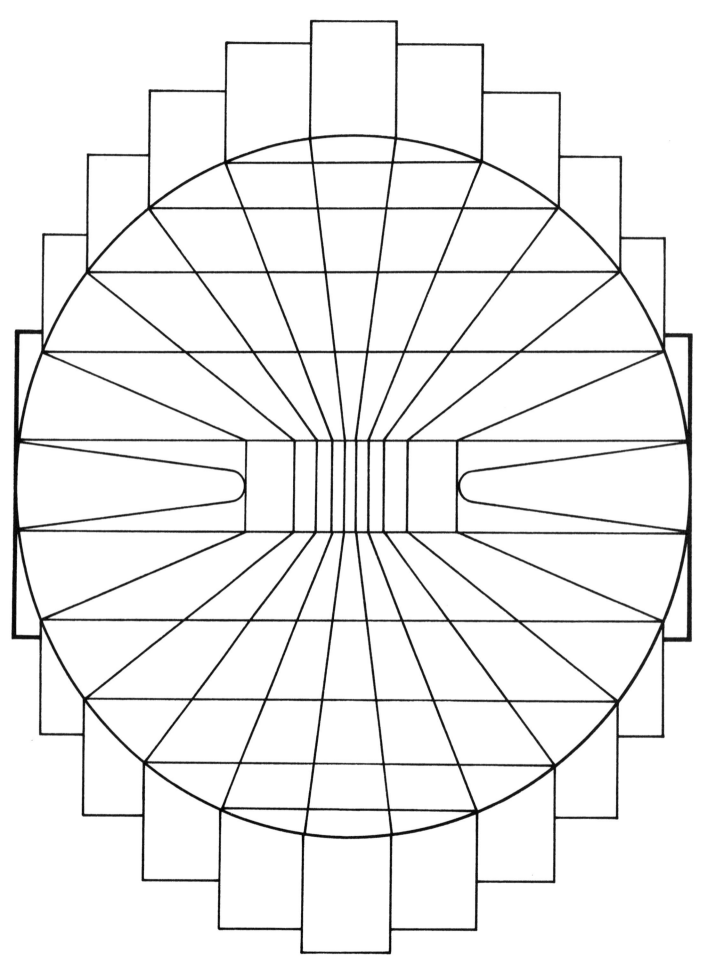

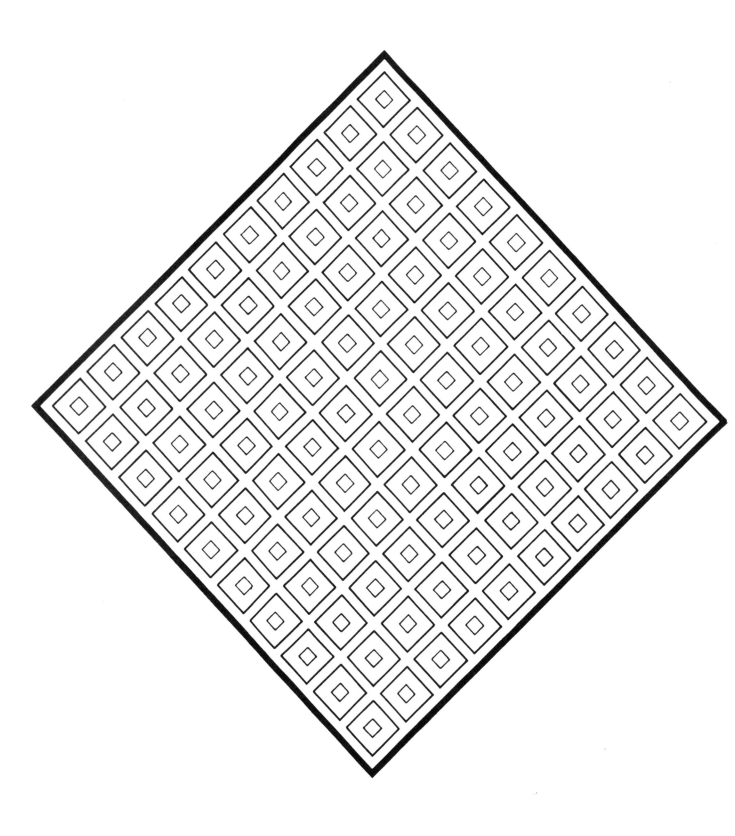

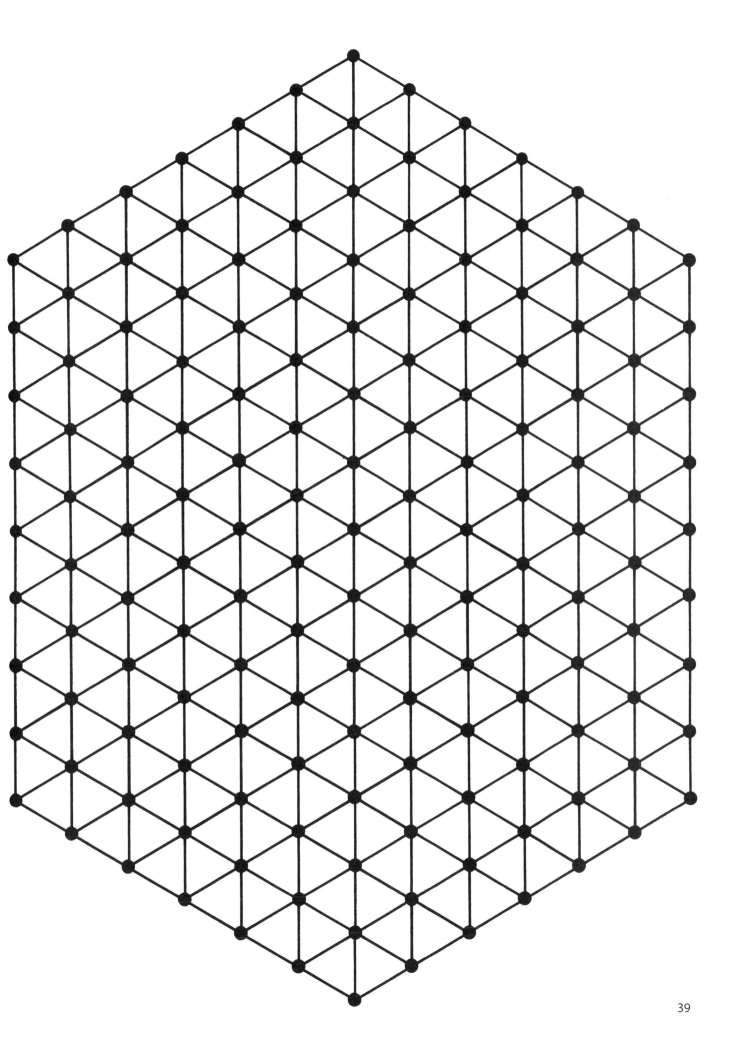

40

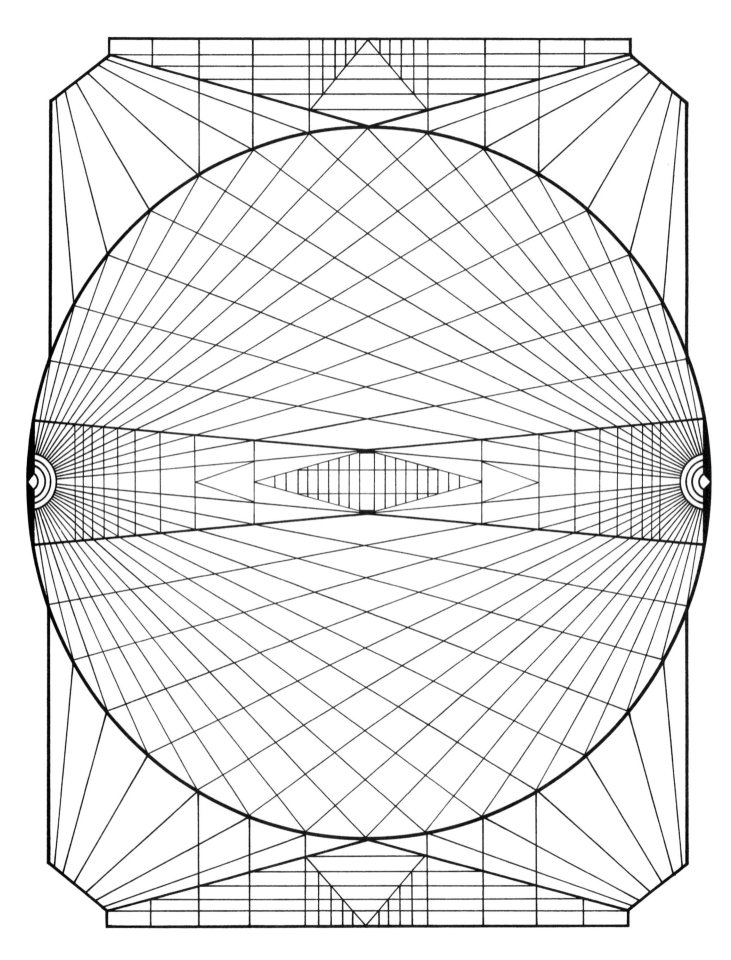

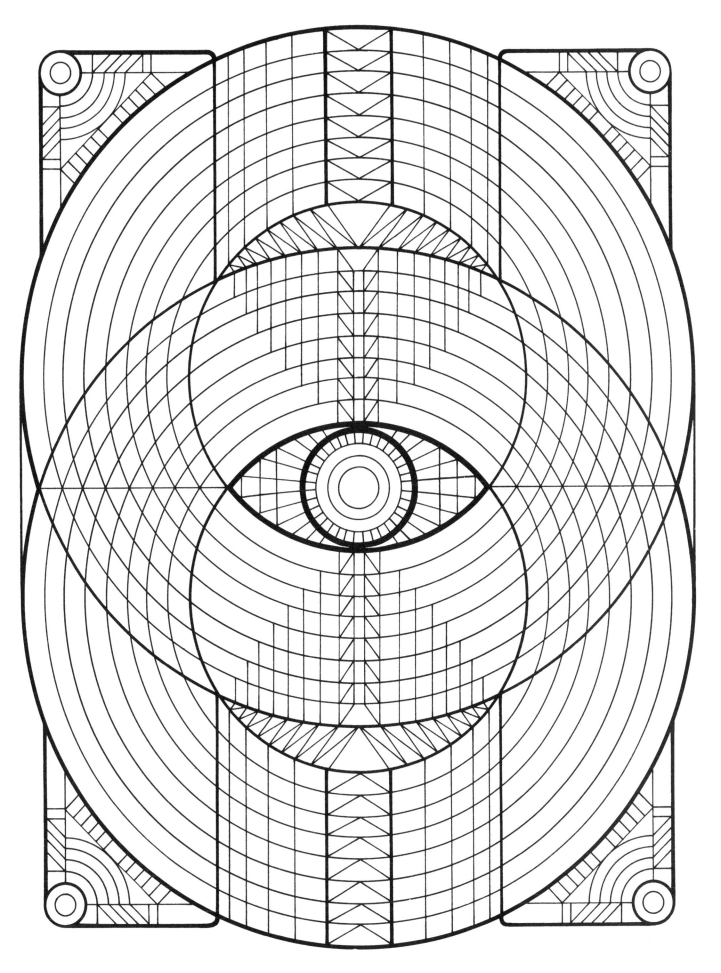

43

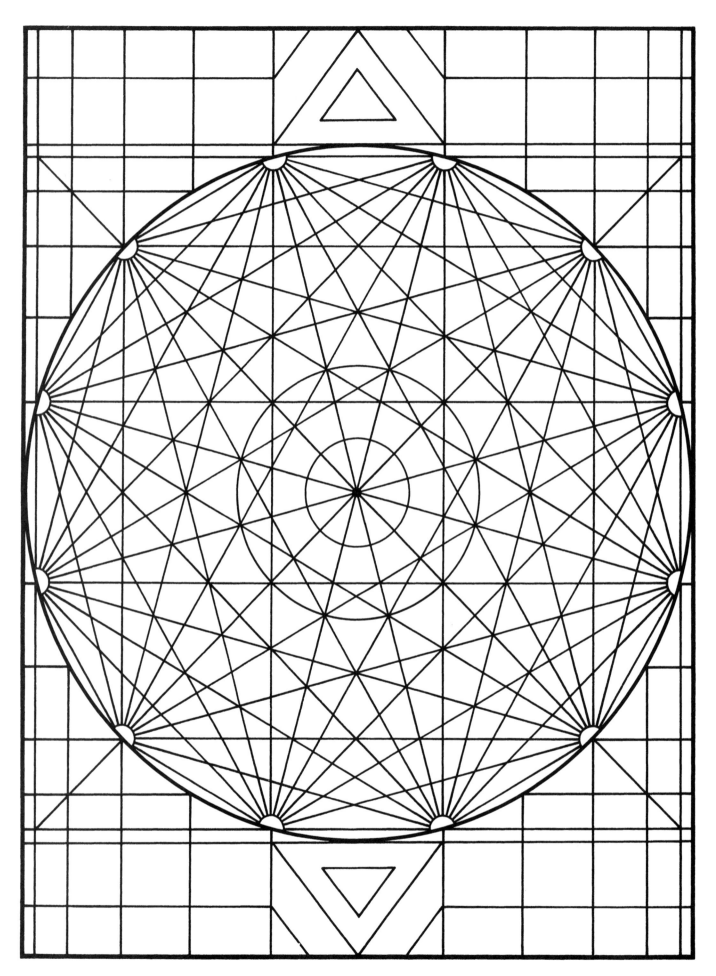

44

45

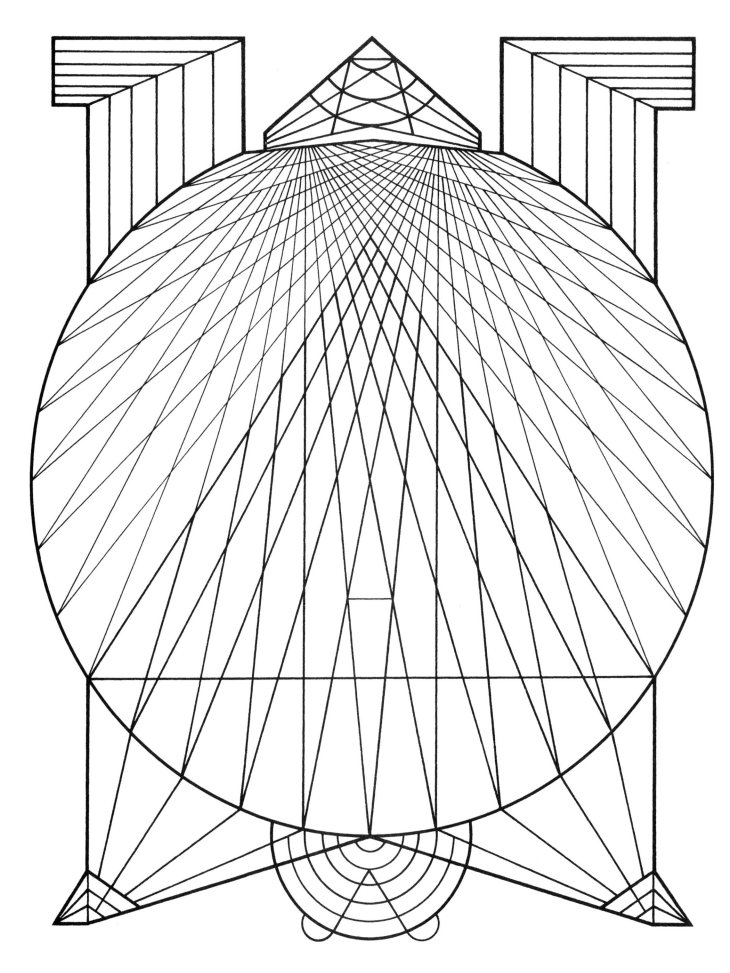

VISUAL ILLUSIONS
Coloring Book

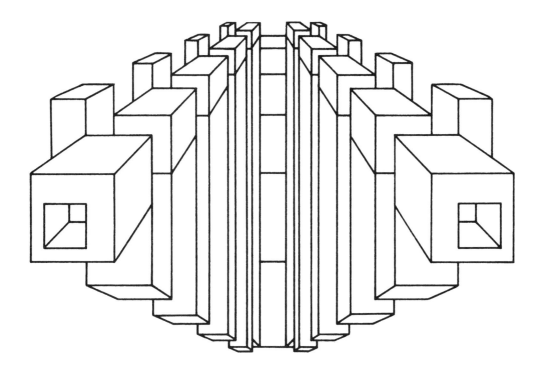

SPYROS HOREMIS

ABOUT THIS BOOK

The visual illusions in this book are geometrical line drawings that take cunning advantage of the nature and habits of our eyes, and persuade them to accept an unreal situation.

In most of the illustrations, the black-and-white line art creates a three-dimensional effect. Amazingly, as you stare at these drawings, "top" and "bottom" and "in" and "out" change places before your eyes! And often the solid object suggested could not possibly exist even in *three* dimensions.

Coloring these drawings is challenging and fun. You have the freedom and opportunity to enhance the illusion greatly by a careful selection and distribution of a wide variety of colors. And, the possibilities are endless!

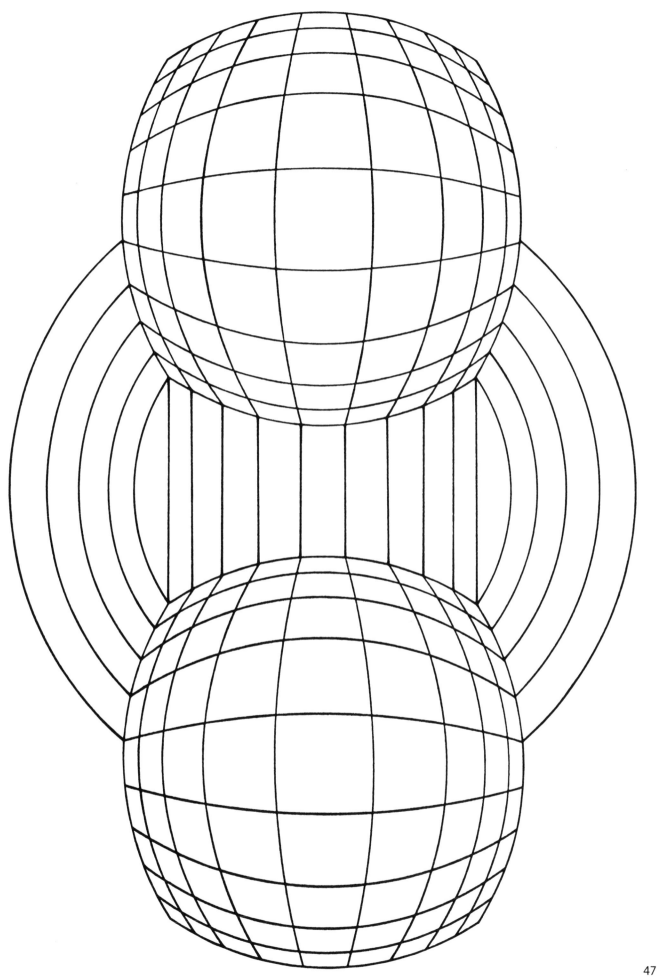

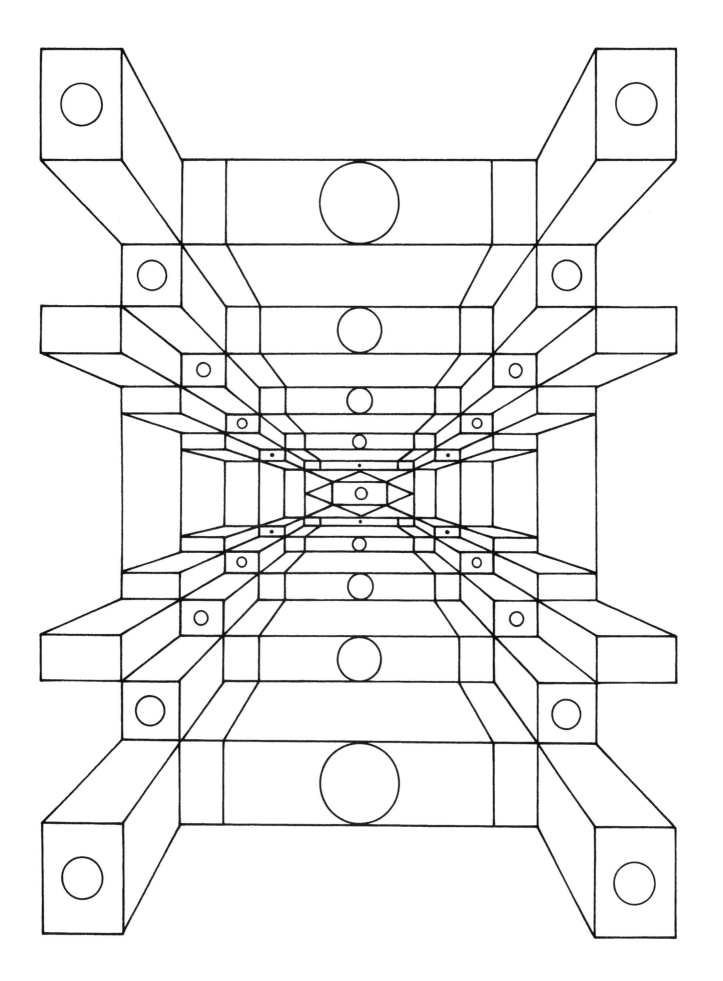

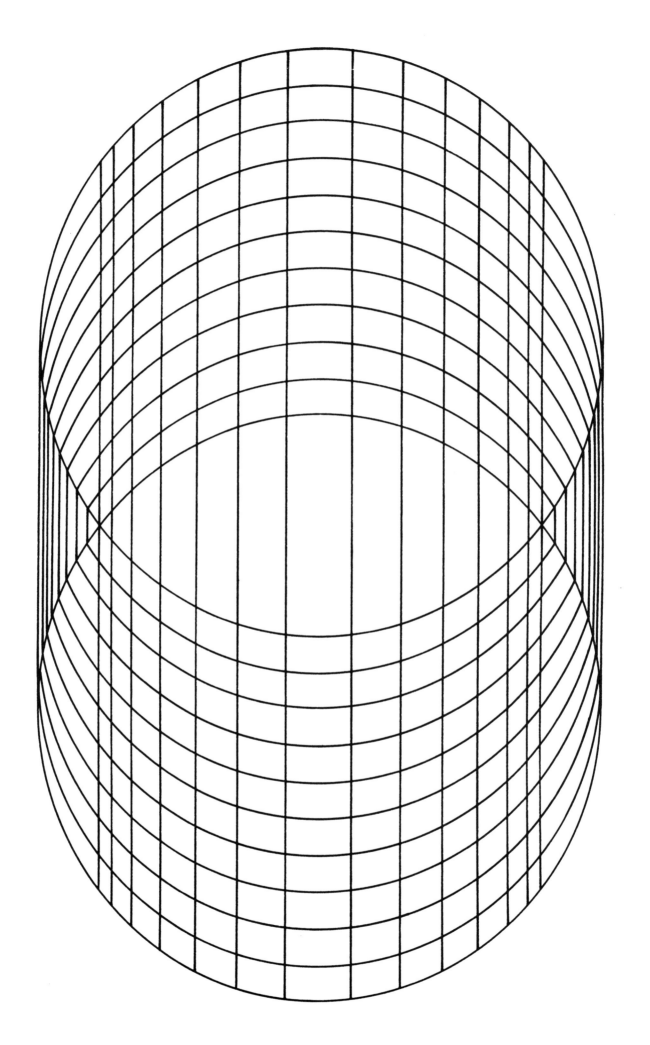

52

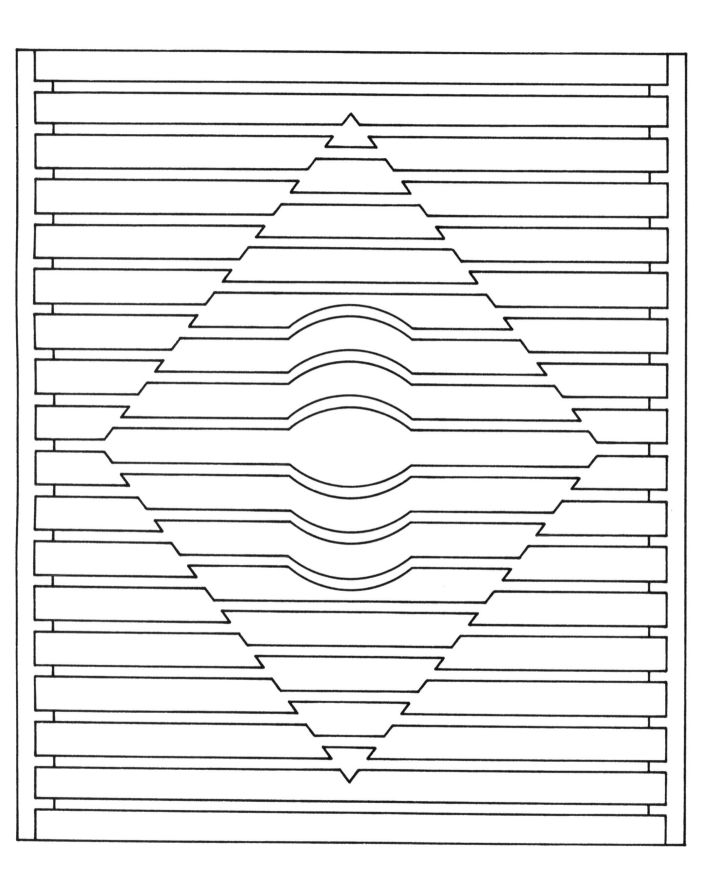

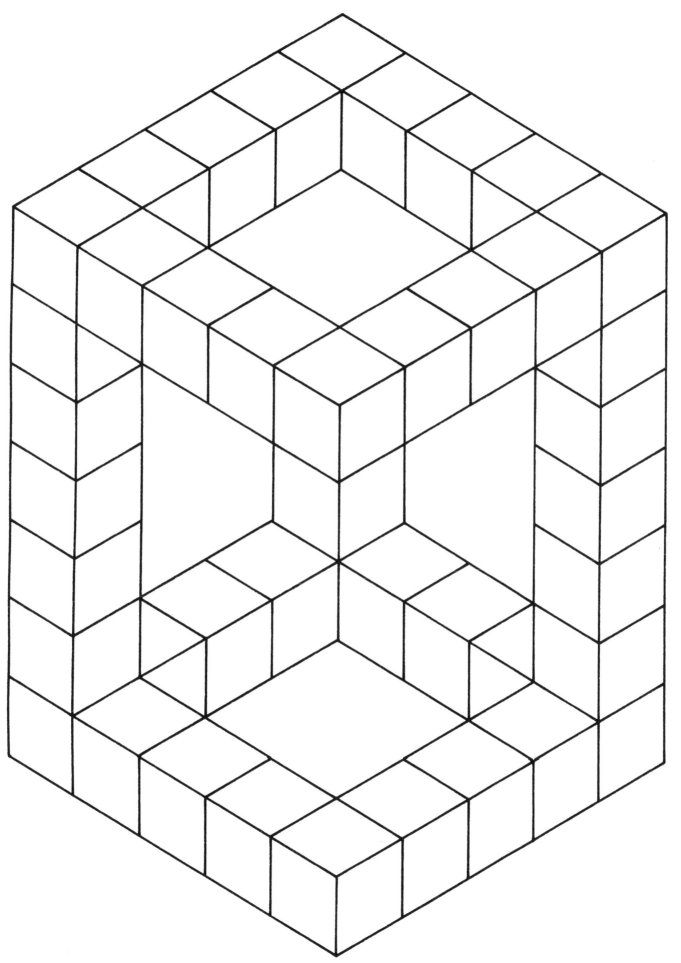

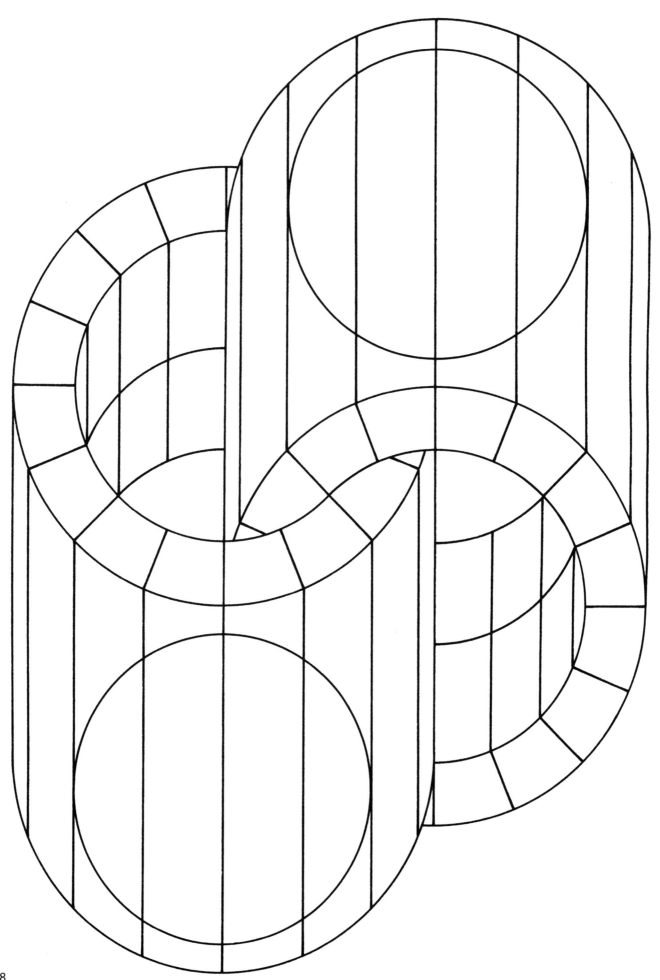

58

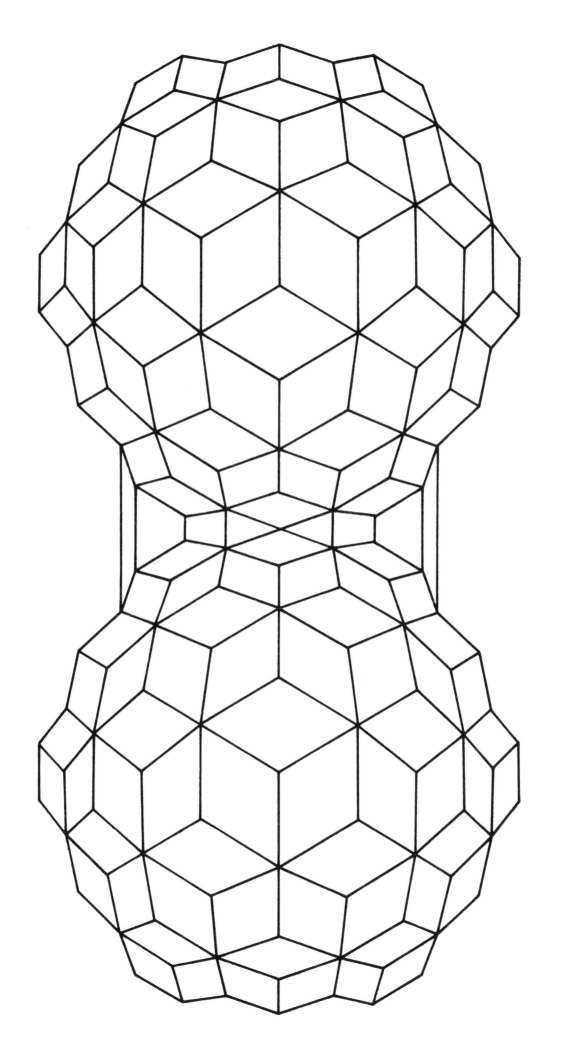

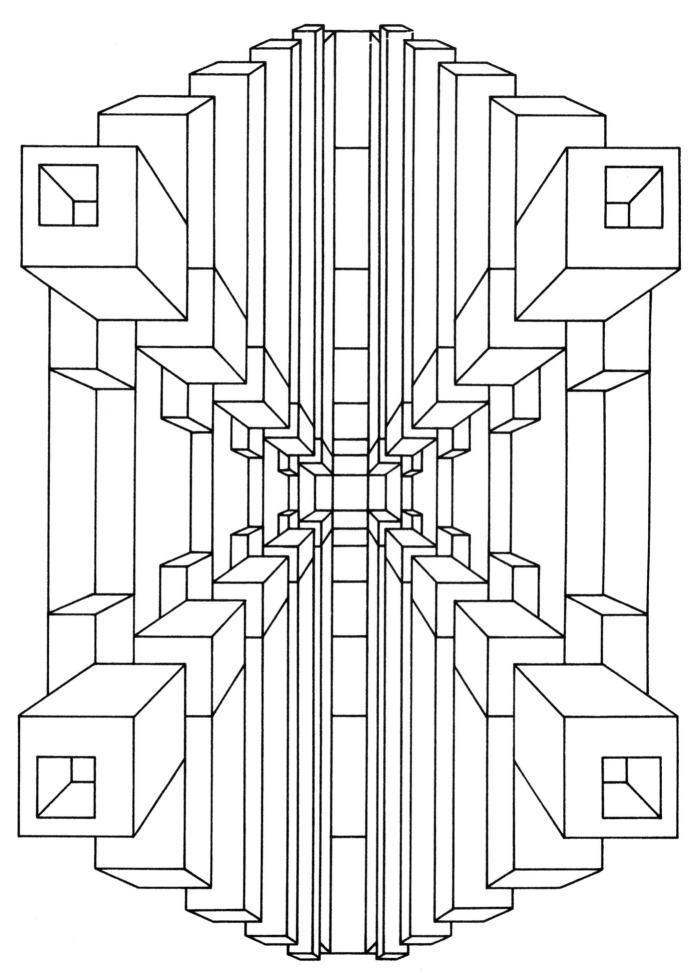

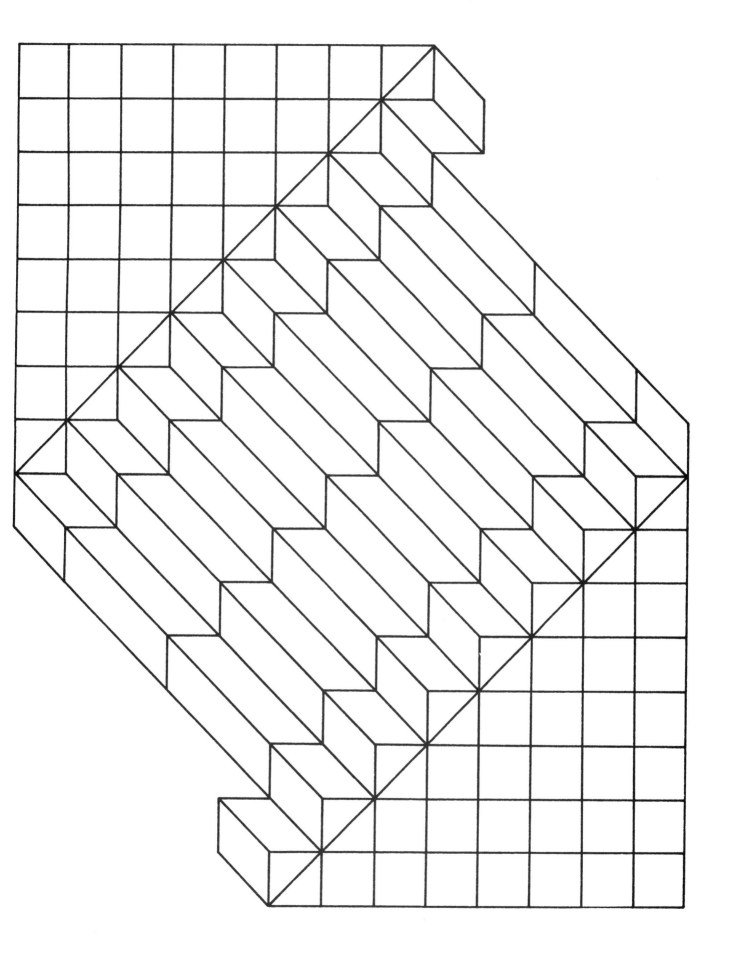

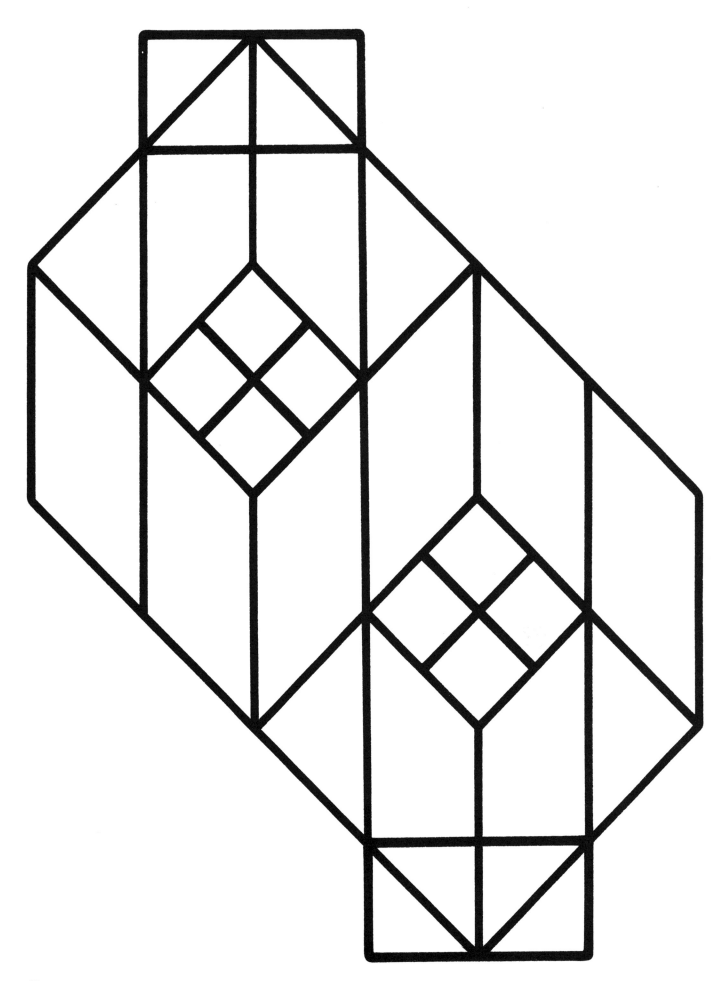

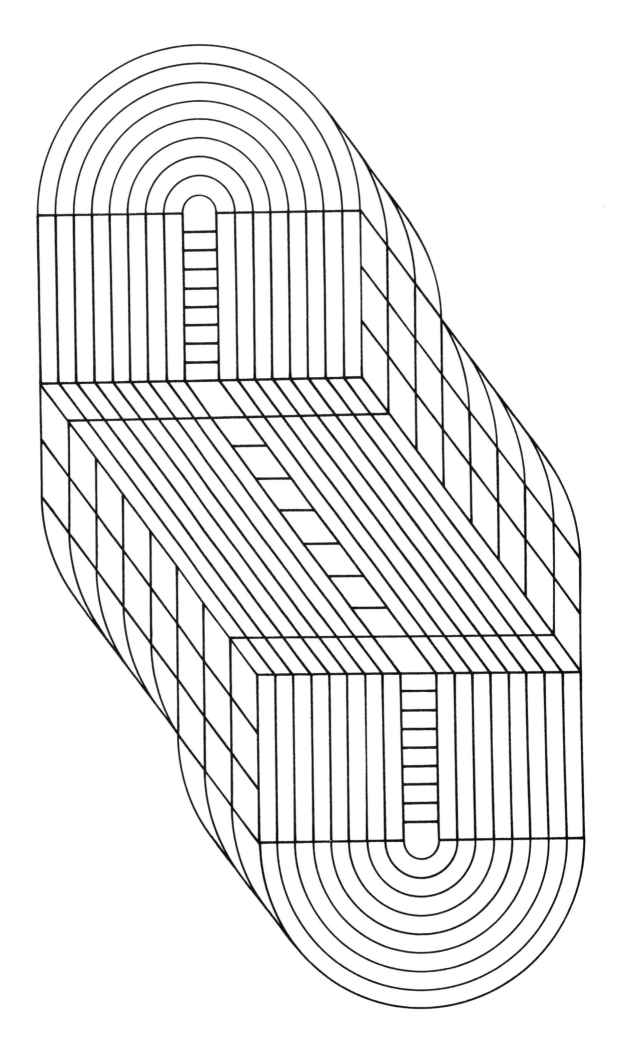

64

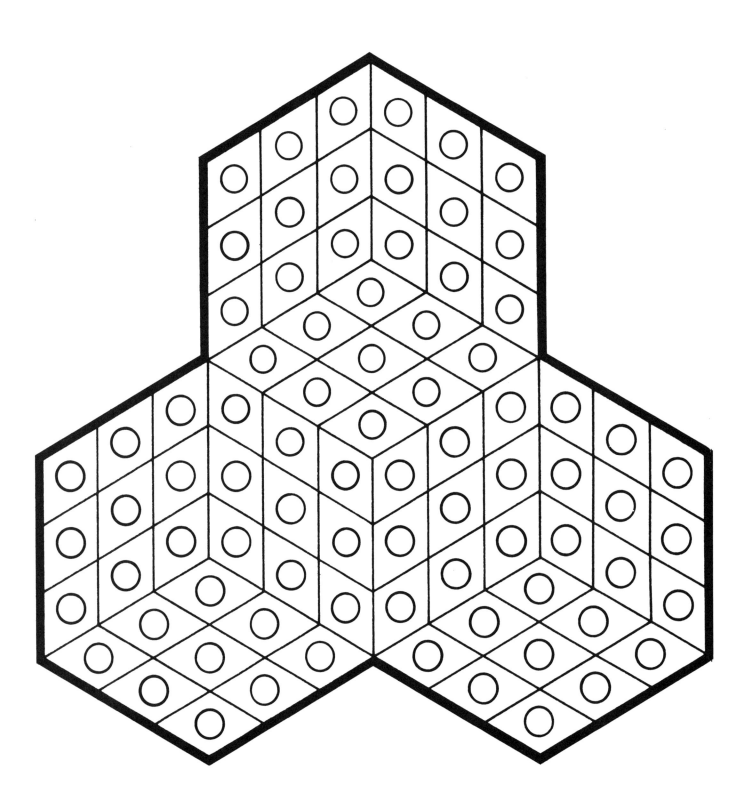

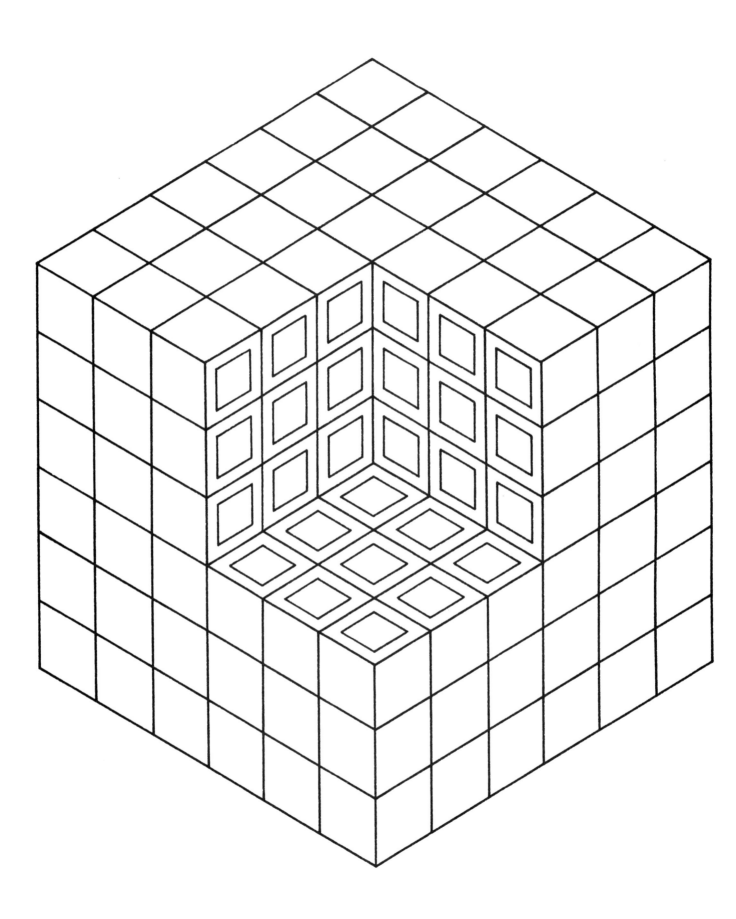

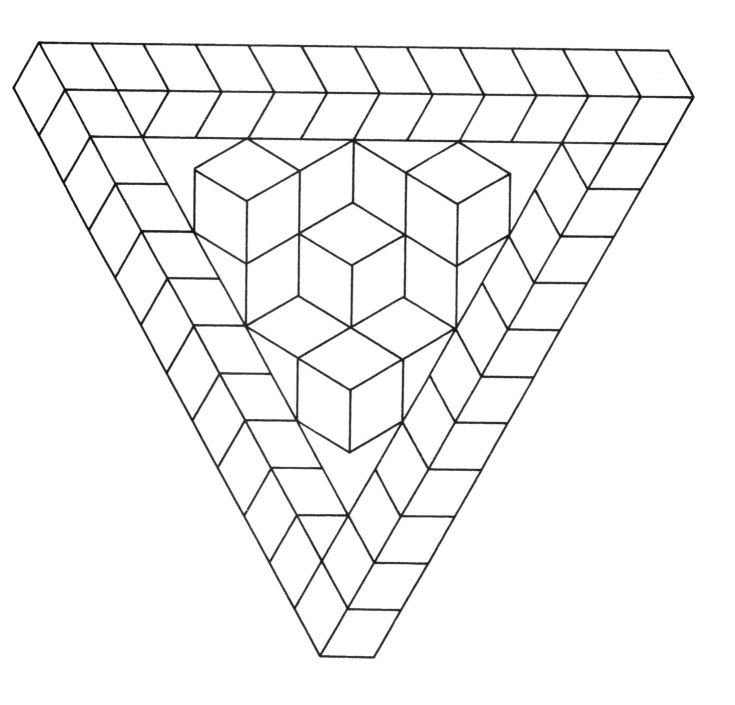

74

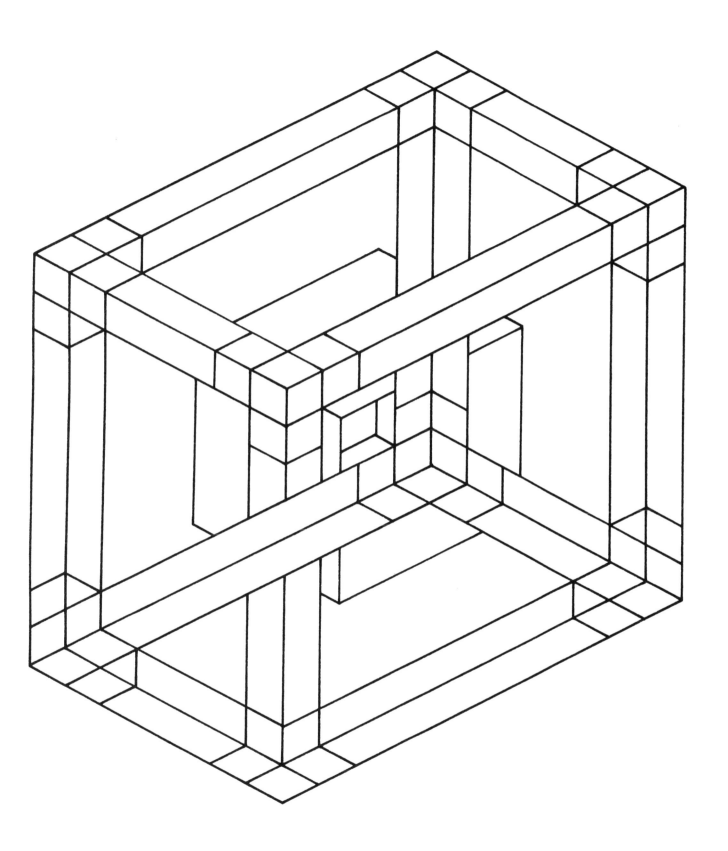

DAZZLING DESIGNS
Coloring Book

KOICHI SATO

ABOUT THIS BOOK

This coloring book is another product of the fertile visual imagination of the graphic artist Koichi Sato. Untethered to the coloring conventions dictated by representations of actual objects, these images present unlimited possibilities to the colorist. It is impossible to make a "wrong" choice. Use whatever color scheme you wish, and the finished design will be uniquely your own. No one else—not even the original artist—will have seen it the way you have!

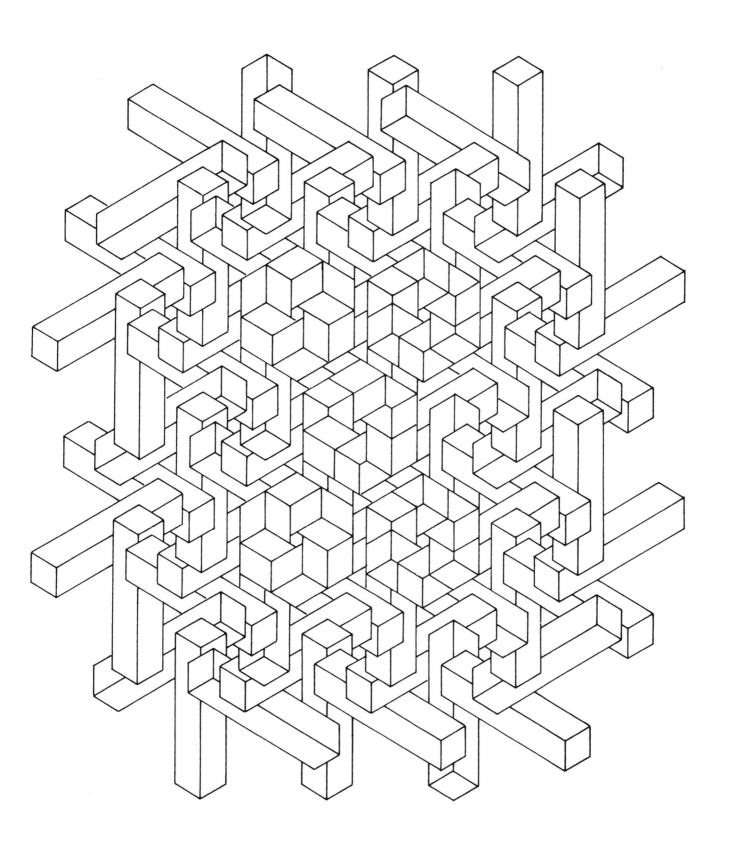

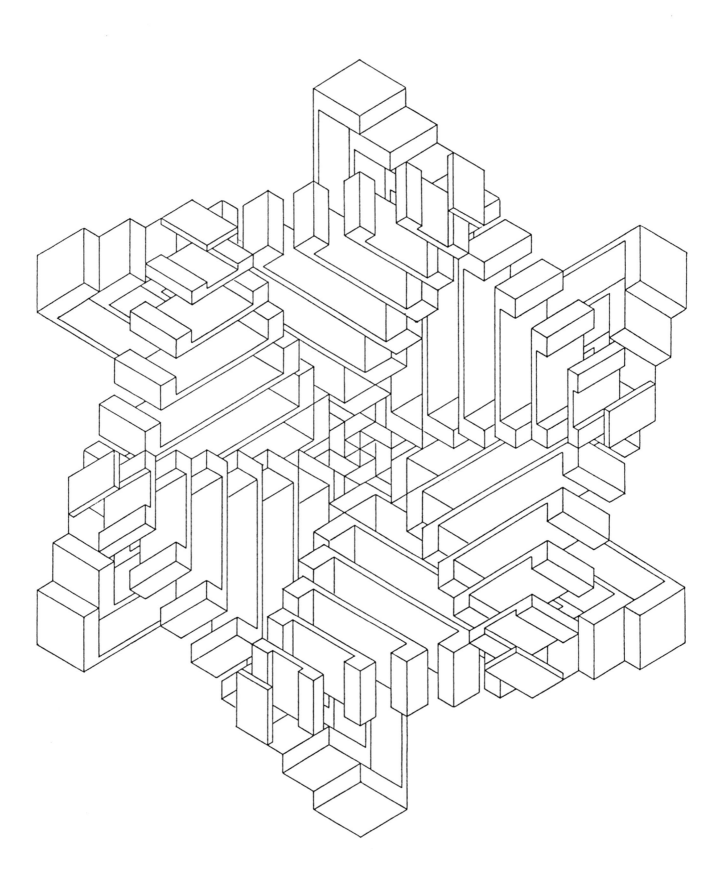

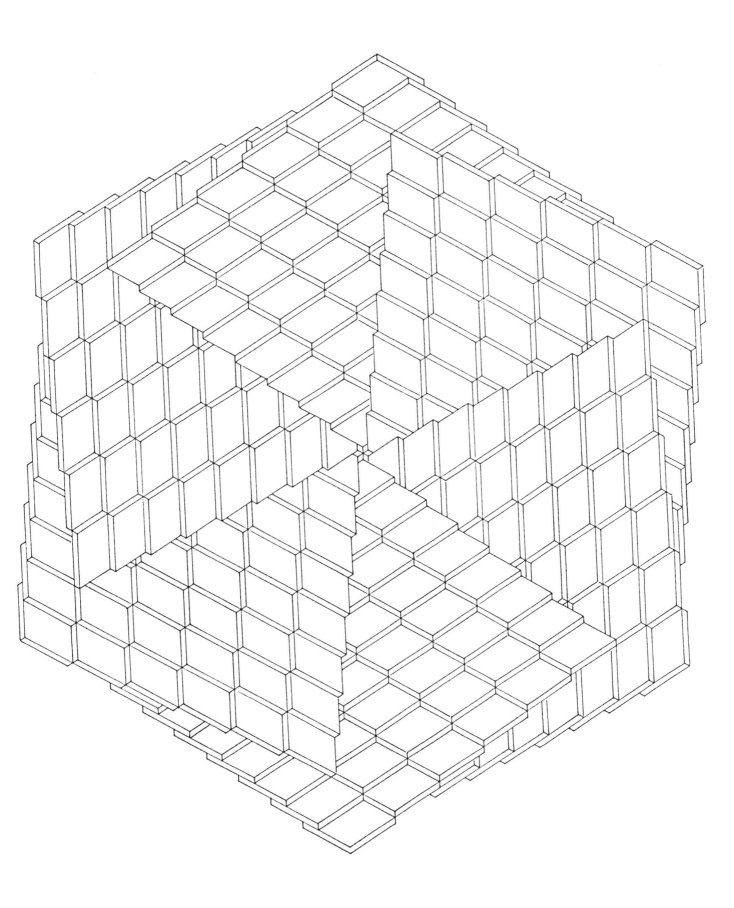

88

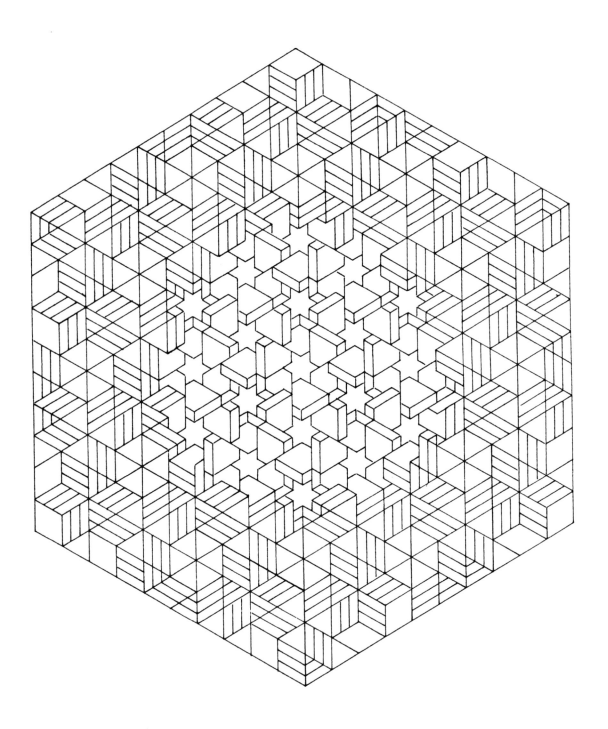

94

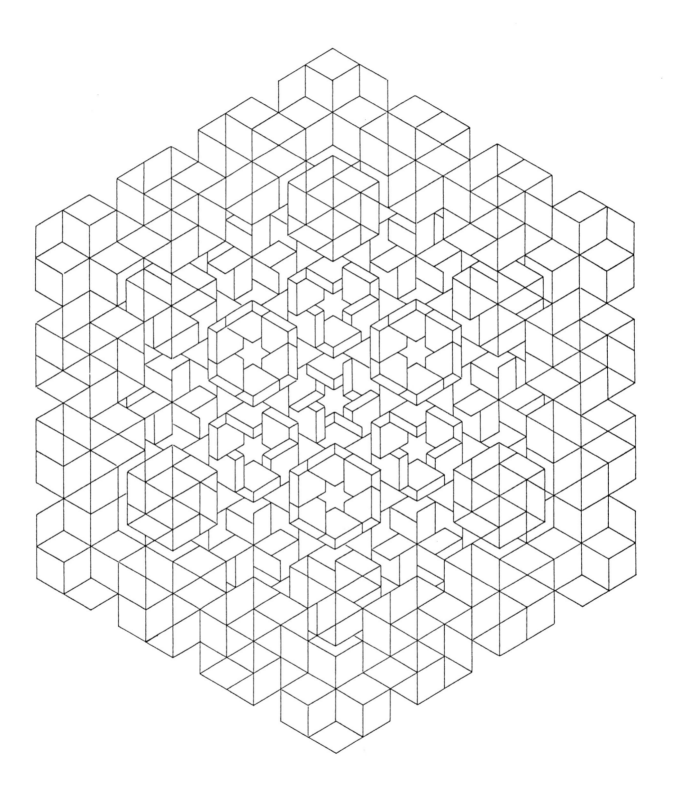

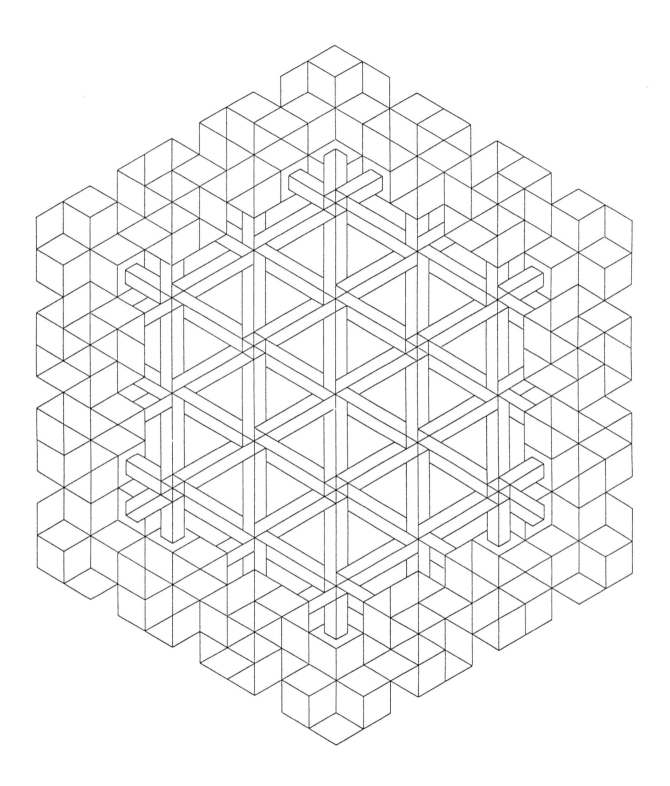

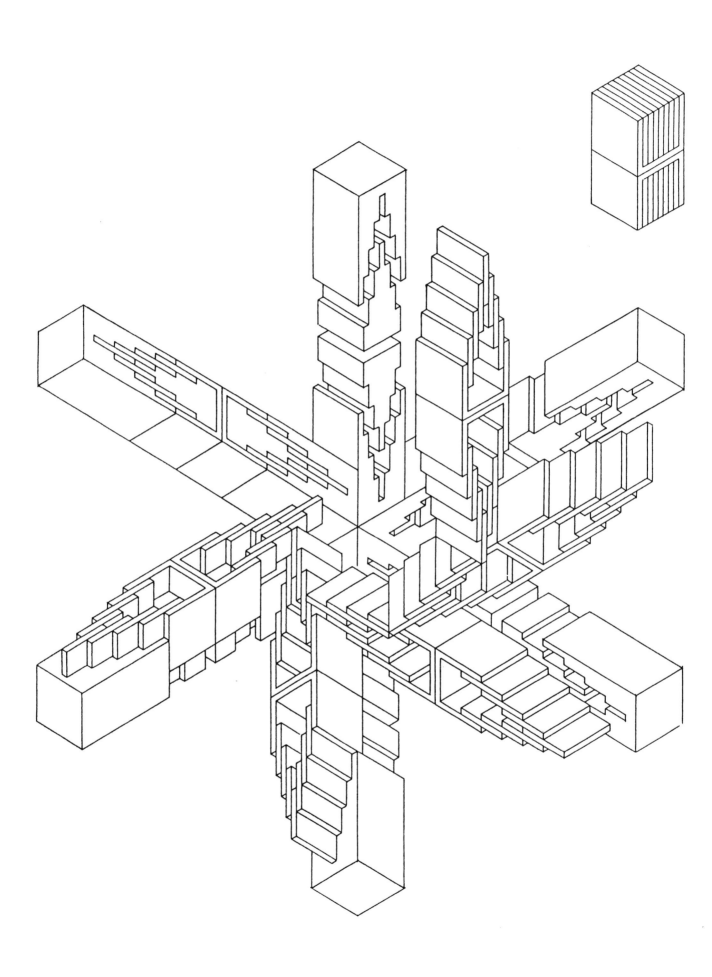

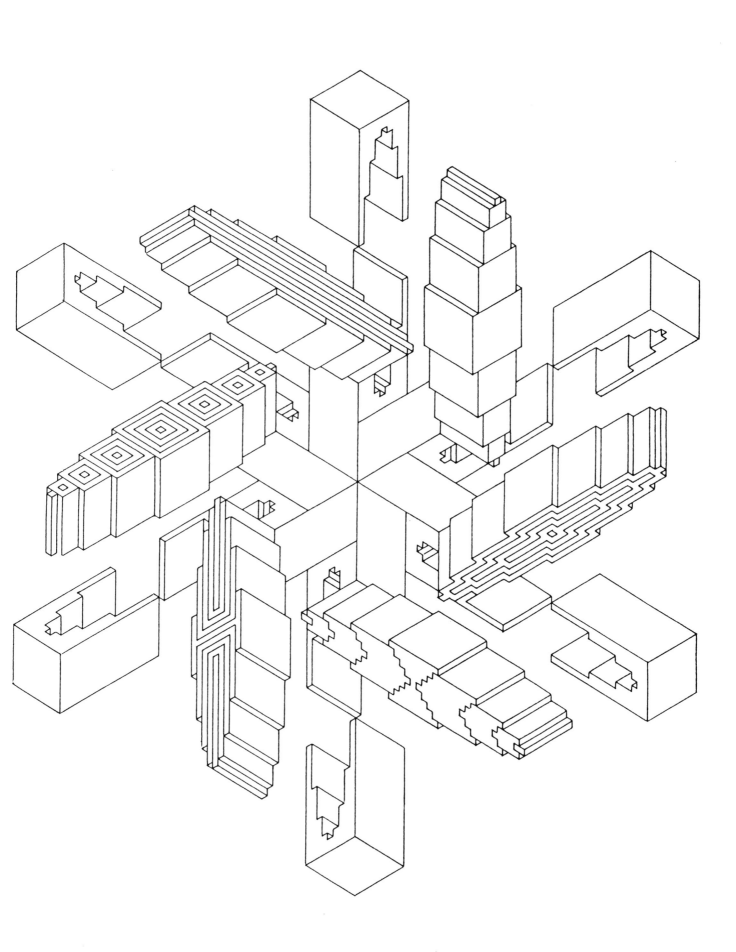

OPTICAL ILLUSIONS
Coloring Book

KOICHI SATO

ABOUT THIS BOOK

This coloring book of optical illusions presents 30 brain-bending geometric designs by graphic artist Koichi Sato. Preying upon conventional notions of space and perspective, these patterns create dazzling visual paradoxes when examined.

These images present unlimited coloring possibilities. You may wish to carefully contrast the colors of different areas to maximize the optical effects of the patterns. However you choose to color them, these designs are sure to create striking and puzzling effects.

107

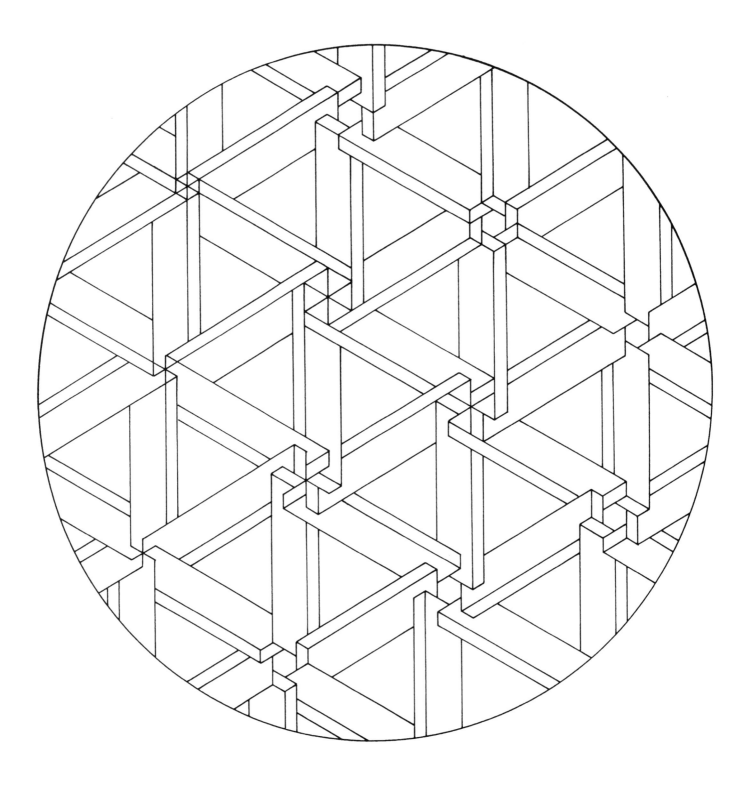

110

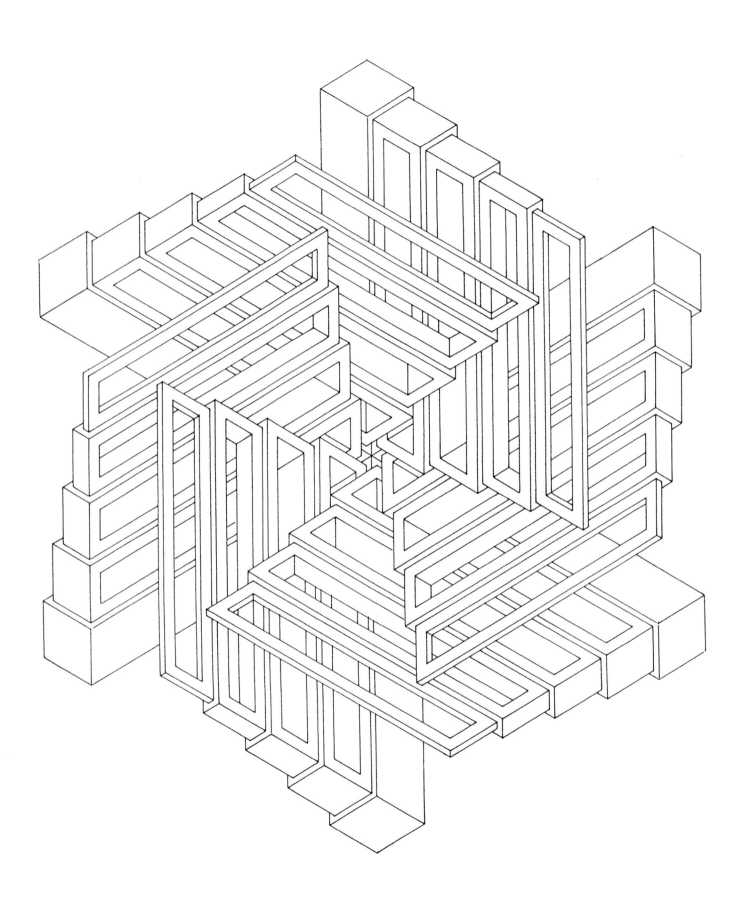

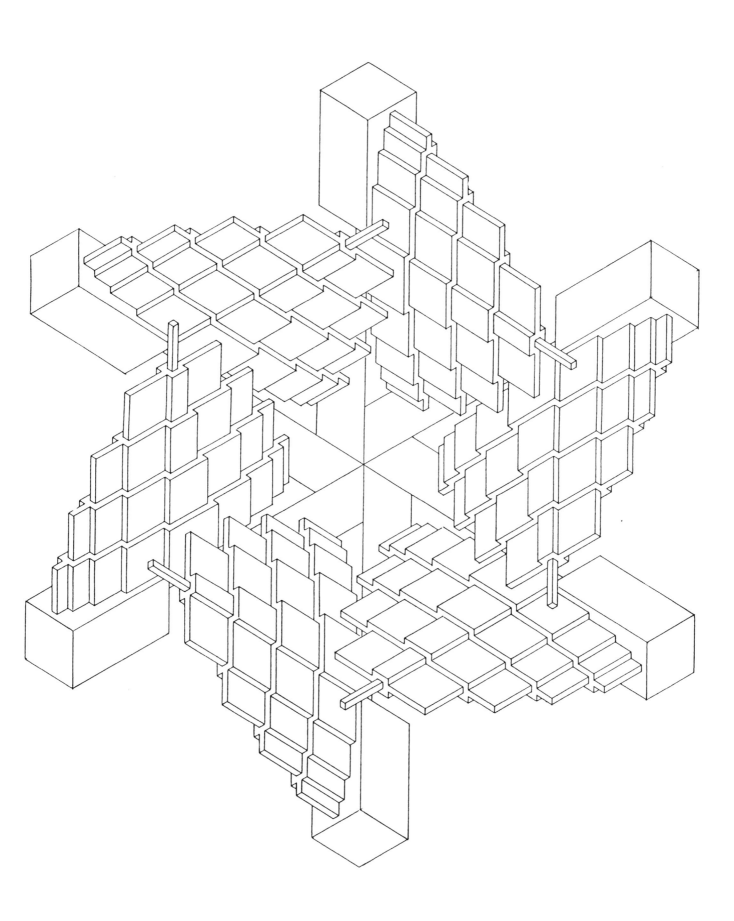

114

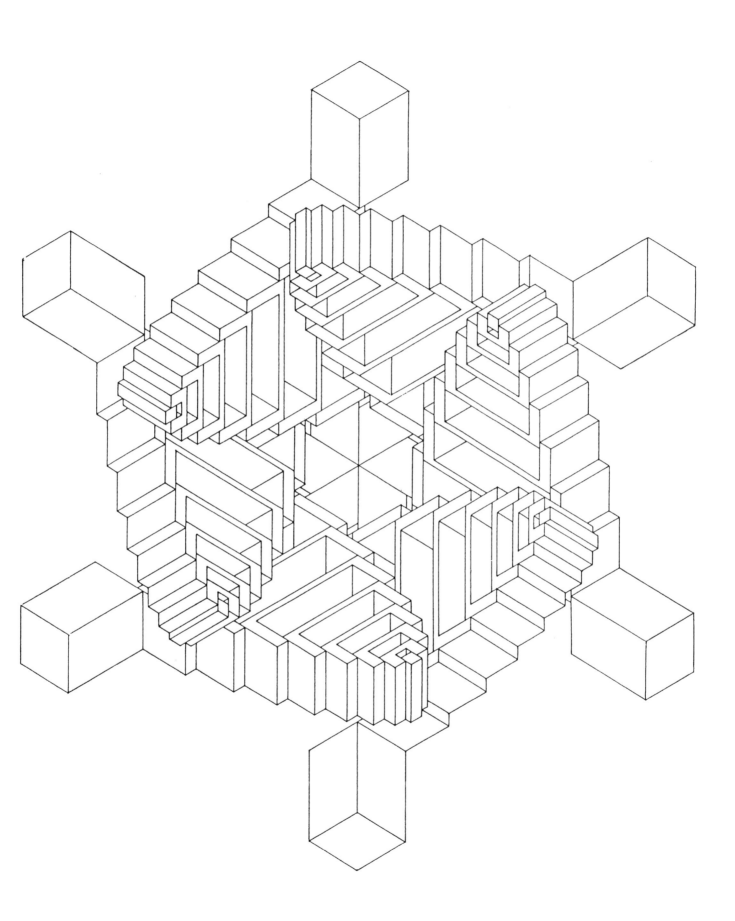

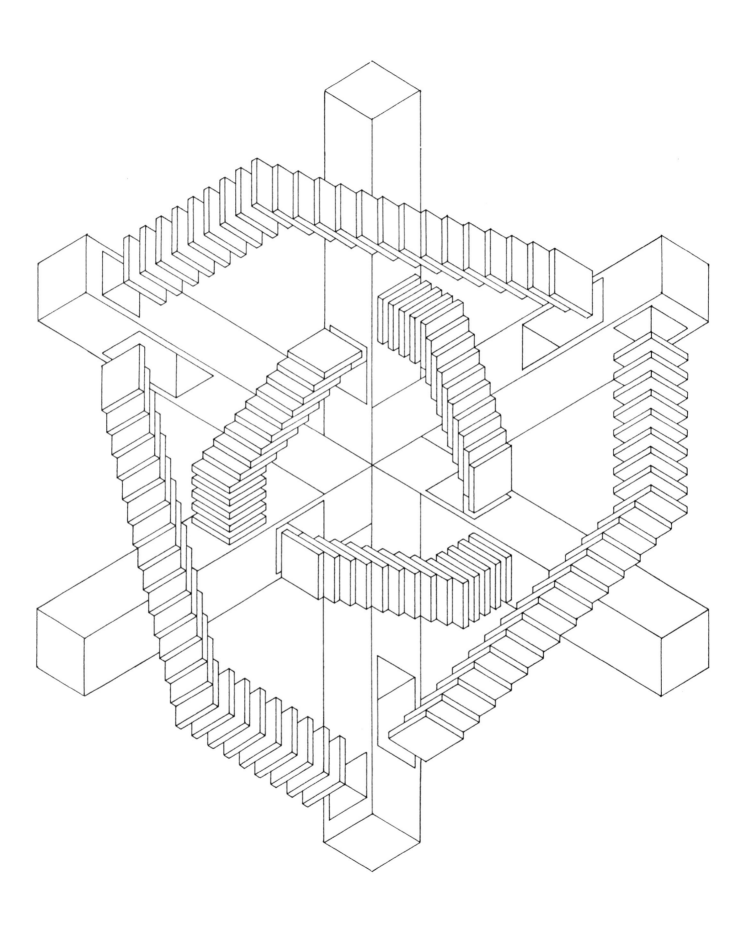

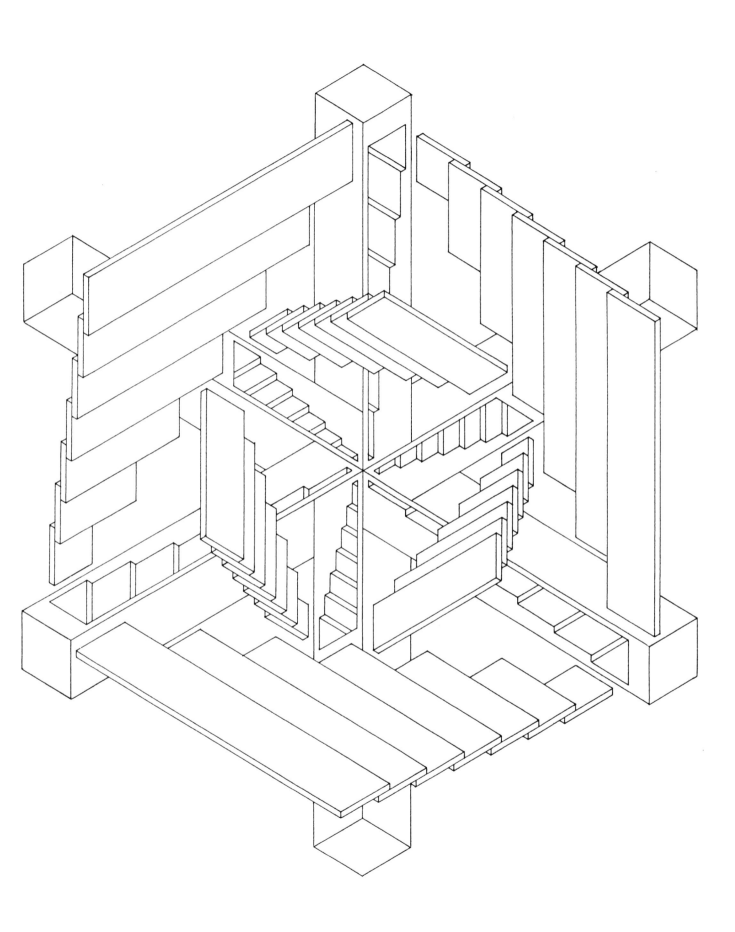

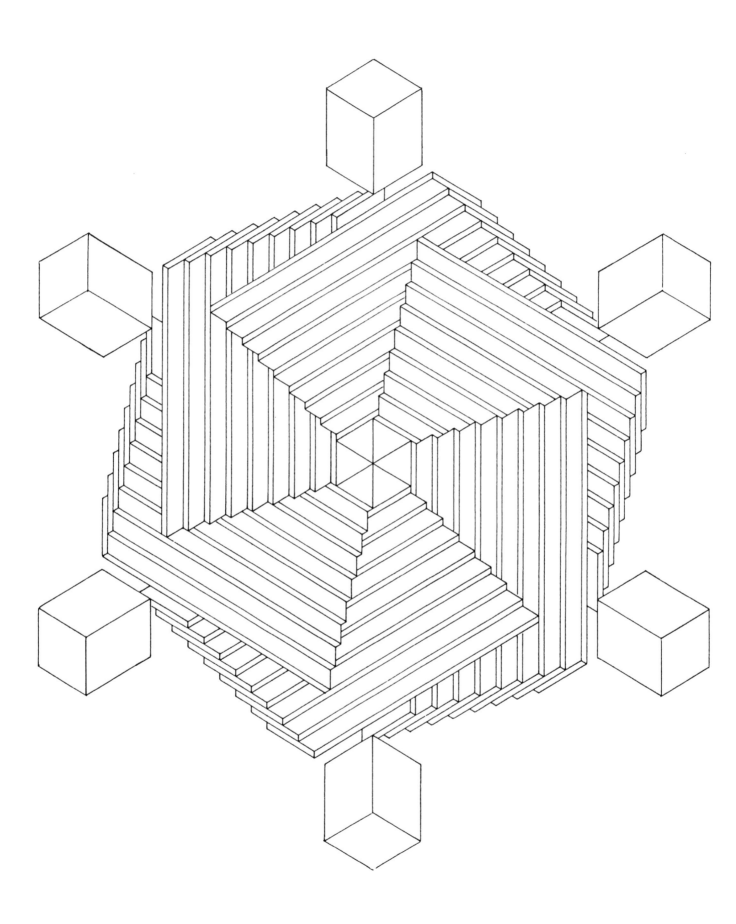

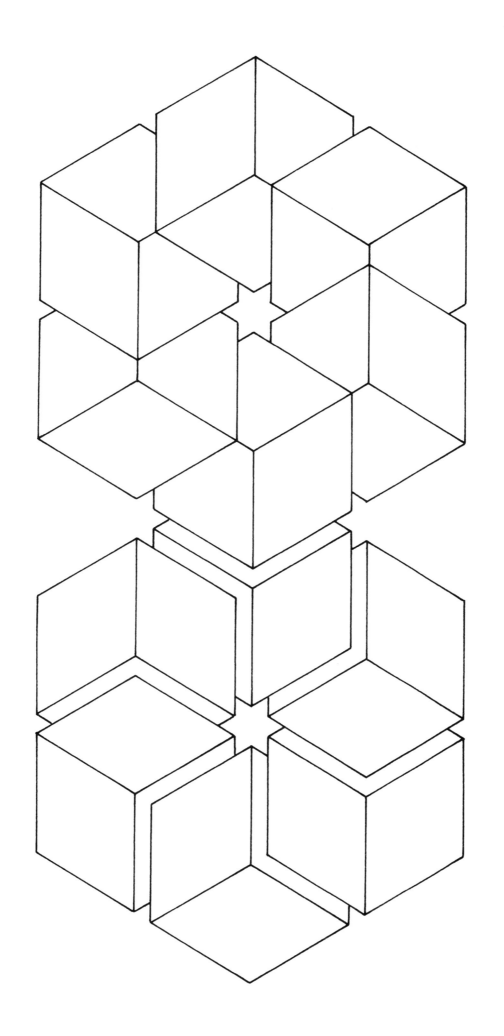

134